PRAYER AND
STUDY GUIDE

TH
POWE
OF
Praying™
Together

STORMIE
OMARTIAN

HARVEST HOUSE™ PUBLISHERS

EUGENE, OREGON

Cover by Koechel Peterson & Associates, Minneapolis, Minnesota

Based on material from *The Power of Praying™ Together* with Jack Hayford.

Harvest House Publishers, Inc., is the exclusive licensee of the trademark THE POWER OF PRAYING.

THE POWER OF PRAYING™ TOGETHER PRAYER AND STUDY GUIDE
Copyright © 2003 by Stormie Omartian
Published by Harvest House Publishers
Eugene, Oregon 97402
www.harvesthousepublishers.com

Library of Congress Cataloging-in-Publication Data

ISBN 0-7369-1007-7

Printed in the United States of America.

03 04 05 06 07 08 09 10 11 / BC-KB / 10 9 8 7 6 5 4 3 2 1

A supplemental workbook to
THE POWER OF PRAYING TOGETHER
by Stormie Omartian with Jack Hayford,
for in-depth group or individual study.

Contents

Where
Do I Start?

This PRAYER AND STUDY GUIDE will help you to understand the power of praying with other believers and motivate you to incorporate that as a regular practice in your life. It will also encourage you to identify and tap into the rich resource of opportunity around you to pray with others concerning the issues and people you care about and the world you live in.

What You Will Need

All you need is the book THE POWER OF PRAYING TOGETHER and a Bible you can write in. The New King James Version is used in this book, but other translations will work as well.

How to Proceed

This PRAYER AND STUDY GUIDE is divided into 14 weeks, which is two weeks on each chapter of the book. Read half of the chapter as indicated for the week, and complete the corresponding questions in the PRAYER AND STUDY GUIDE. If you are meeting with a group, the leader will go over each question to see what insight God has given you. If you are not involved in group study, you can go over these questions on your own. I pray they will motivate you to deepen your prayer commitment, grow in your intimate prayer walk with God, and take advantage of opportunities to pray with others whenever possible.

Read Chapter 1(a) : "What Is the Power and
How Do I Get It?" (pages 13-28) from
THE POWER OF PRAYING TOGETHER

1. Read 1 Corinthians 1:18 and underline it in your Bible.
   What is the message of the cross to an unbeliever? ___
   _____.
   What is the message of the cross to those who believe
   in Jesus and have received Him as their Savior? _____
   _____.
   What does this mean for you personally?

2. Read Matthew 16:19 in your Bible and underline it.
   According to this verse, Jesus has given authority to His
   people to do what? _____
   _____.
   Keys mean the _____, the _____, the
   _____. The key doesn't _____ the power of
   the engine, it _____ the _____ of

9

the engine. (See page 22, top of page, in THE POWER OF PRAYING TOGETHER.)

3. Read John 1:12 in your Bible and underline it. If you have received Jesus as your Savior, what does this verse mean to you? _____
_____. If you had an earthly father who gave you keys to a car, that would mean you had a right to that car. If your heavenly Father gives you the keys to His kingdom, what does that mean to you as His child? (See page 22, first complete paragraph, in THE POWER OF PRAYING TOGETHER.)

4. Just as having the keys to a car means that we have responsibility for it, having the keys to God's kingdom means that we are responsible for it too. We are responsible for *our* side of the _____ with God in _____. If we don't use the ___ of _____, then _____ is likely to happen. There won't be anything _____ or _____. (See page 22, second paragraph, of THE POWER OF PRAYING TOGETHER.)

5. Do you ever forget that you have the key, which is prayer, that unlocks God's power? ___. If you answered yes, write out a prayer asking God to help you remember to always make prayer the first thing you do in every situation and not a last resort. If you answered no, write out a prayer asking God to keep you from ever forgetting to make prayer the first thing you do in every situation that arises.

6. Read Isaiah 40:29 in your Bible and underline it. What do you need to see happen in your life that you know won't happen unless God moves in power? Write this as a prayer to God listing all the areas where you especially need to see Him move in power on your behalf. (For example, "Lord, I need to see You move in power in my life in the area of my health...my finances...my relationships...")

7. Read 2 Peter 1:2-3 in your Bible and underline these verses. Where do we find all things that pertain to life and godliness? _____ _____. List below some of the things you would like to see happen in your life or situation that you know can't happen without God's intervening power.

8. Read 2 Corinthians 12:9 in your Bible and underline it. Do you ever feel weak in the midst of your circumstances? ___. In light of this Scripture, why is the fact that you feel weak not something to be concerned about? _____ _____. What do you feel are your weaknesses, and why do you not have to feel badly about them?

9. Read 2 Timothy 3:1-5 in your Bible and underline these verses. Write out a prayer asking God to help you to not be a partaker of any of those things listed in this section of Scripture. Ask Him to help you to not live "having a form of godliness but denying its power." (For example, "Lord, help me to not be a lover of myself, nor a lover of money...")

10. Read 2 Corinthians 13:3-4 in your Bible and underline these verses. According to them, Jesus was crucified in weakness, but He lives by _____ _____. Even though we are weak, we live by that same power too. Write out a prayer thanking God that because Jesus was raised up in power and is mighty in you, you will be raised up in that same power.

11. Read Luke 24:49 in your Bible and underline it. What was Jesus telling His disciples to do? _____ _____ _____.
Have you ever prayed a prayer that felt powerless to you? _____. Explain. Write out a prayer asking God to give you a fresh flow of His Spirit each day so that you can always pray in power.

12. God makes His power available to us to do two
    important things:

    One is to _____
    _____. The
    other is to _____
    _____. But we
    can't do either of those things if we _____
    _____.

    (See page 25, first paragraph, in THE POWER OF PRAYING
    TOGETHER.)

13. Can you think of any way in which you are trying to
    live without the enabling power of God? _____. If you
    answered yes, explain and write out a prayer asking
    God to help you depend on Him as the source of
    power in your life. If you answered no, write out a
    prayer asking God to show you any way in which you
    are trying to depend on your own strength instead of
    relying on His power.

14. Read Ephesians 1:15-21 in your Bible and underline verses 19-21. What did Paul pray for the Ephesians to know in verse 19? What do these verses reveal to you about the power of God with regard to your own life?

15. Write out a prayer thanking God that His power is mighty *in* you and great *toward* you. Acknowledge that without the power of the Holy Spirit flowing *through* you, you can't accomplish anything that is lasting or significant. Ask Him to make you like a lightning rod as you transmit His power in prayer. (See page 28, second paragraph, in THE POWER OF PRAYING TOGETHER.)

Read Chapter 1(b): "What Is the Power and
How Do I Get It?" (pages 28-37) from
THE POWER OF PRAYING TOGETHER

+1. Read Mark 6:46-48 in your Bible and underline these
   verses. What did Jesus do before He walked on water
   to meet His disciples in the boat? _____
   _____. What do these verses say to
   you in terms of what *you* should do in order to see the
   power of God move in your life? _____.
   Write out a prayer asking God to help you live like
   Jesus and always seek God first.

+2. Read Luke 6:12-19 in your Bible and underline verses
   12 and 19. Where did Jesus go to be infused with
   power? _____
   (verse 12). What did He accomplish immediately after
   that time? _____
   (verse 19). Jesus spent intimate time with His heavenly

Father before He did some of His most amazing miracles. Write out a prayer asking God to help you spend quality time in prayer with Him the way Jesus did when He was here on earth.

3. Who is in the driver's seat of your life? Is it you? Is it someone else? Is it the Lord? Explain. (If you don't know, ask God to show you.) Write out a prayer asking God to help you be controlled, led, and empowered by His Holy Spirit.

4. Read Philippians 2:5-8 in your Bible and underline these verses. Even though Jesus was God, what did He choose to do? _____

_____

_____ (verse 7).
In light of this section of Scripture, what should you choose to do as well? _____

_____ (verse 8).

Who should control our minds? _____.
How do you think that happens? _____

_____

_____.

5. What did Jesus not depend on as God? _____
   _____. He was God,
   but He chose to walk as what? _____.
   When God became flesh, He laid aside His divinity
   and became what? _____

   _____.

   When He did all this, did He do it willingly? _____. Did
   He ever become less than God? _____. (See page 29,
   first paragraph, in THE POWER OF PRAYING TOGETHER.)

6. When we pray, "Your kingdom come," we are asking
   God's _____ to invade _____ _____
   right now. (See page 30, first paragraph, in THE POWER
   OF PRAYING TOGETHER.) Even though Jesus was the Son
   of God, He still went to ____ _____ in _____
   in order to receive _____ for all He needed to
   do. And He teaches us how to ____ ____ _____.
   God wants us to draw on ____ _____
   by coming to Him in _____ and seeking a
   _____ _____ of _____
   the way _____ did. (See page 29, second
   paragraph, in THE POWER OF PRAYING TOGETHER.)

7. Read Matthew 6:9-13 in your Bible and underline these verses. When you pray this prayer, what are the things you are asking God to do *today?* List them below.

8. Just like Jesus, we need to be empowered by the Holy Spirit in all that we do. In what ways do you need to be empowered by the Holy Spirit? (See page 30, second paragraph, in THE POWER OF PRAYING TOGETHER for suggestions.)

9. Read Luke 10:19-20 in your Bible and underline these two verses. What did Jesus say was the most important thing to rejoice over? _____
_____.

Why is that important for you to remember? _____
_____.

(See page 31, second paragraph, in THE POWER OF PRAYING TOGETHER.) Write out a prayer thanking God that your name is written in heaven.

10. Have you ever been a crisis "pray-er"? _____.
(See page 32, first paragraph, in THE POWER OF PRAYING TOGETHER.) Do you find yourself praying far more in a time of crisis than you would at any other time? _____. What should you do ongoingly with regard to prayer? Why? (See the second paragraph.)

11. The kingdom of God is what? _____
_____. It is also a realm where the reign of God does what? _____
_____. Even though our ultimate destination is with Him in heaven, what is our interim destination? _____
_____
_____. What is pivotal to our

fulfilling God's purpose for us here? _____.
(See page 32, last paragraph, in THE POWER OF PRAYING
TOGETHER.)

12. What is the primary business of God's people?
_____. (See page 33, fourth paragraph, in
THE POWER OF PRAYING TOGETHER.) How well we understand and accept this _____ and
_____ we have in _____
will determine how much of _____
_____ will penetrate our _____.
As Pastor Jack says, "All _____ in heaven
and earth is _____, but all _____ invoking
_____ _____ into earth's
need is _____." (See page 34, first paragraph.)

13. If we invite God's sovereign power to manifest in
earth's suffering and pain, what will happen? (See
page 34, second paragraph, in THE POWER OF PRAYING
TOGETHER.)

14. Read 1 Peter 2:9 in your Bible and underline it. Write out a prayer proclaiming God's praises. Thank Him for everything you can find to thank Him for in this Scripture. Ask Him to help you understand how to appropriate His power in prayer so that His will is done on earth.

15. Pray the prayer on pages 35-36 in THE POWER OF PRAYING TOGETHER out loud. Include specifics about your own life. List below the parts of the prayer you most need God to answer.

Read Chapter 2(a): "The Power of One"
(pages 39-54) from
THE POWER OF PRAYING TOGETHER

1. The more time we spend _____ with _____,
   the more _____ our _____ will
   be when we _____ with _____. (See page
   43, last paragraph, in THE POWER OF PRAYING TOGETHER.)
   Praying with other people without spending _____
   _____ with ___ will compromise the _____
   _____ and _____
   of your _____. In other words, you will be a
   more effective _____ _____ if you have
   not neglected your _____ _____ with the _____.
   (See page 44, top of page.)

2. List six things that prayer is. (See pages 44-46, bold,
   italic print, in THE POWER OF PRAYING TOGETHER.)

   1. Prayer is _communicating with_
      God.

   2. Prayer is _praising + worshipping_
      God for who He is.

3. Prayer is _____
_____.

4. Prayer is _____
_____.

5. Prayer is _____
_____.

6. Prayer is _____
_____.

3. Read Ephesians 2:13 and Hebrews 4:14-16 in your
Bible and underline them. Why do we have the priv-
ilege of communicating with God through prayer?
How are we supposed to come before God?

4. What is the difference between the "fellowship" side
of prayer and the "partnership" side of prayer? Do you
feel that you experience both fellowship and partnership with God in prayer? Explain. (See page 45, first
paragraph, in THE POWER OF PRAYING TOGETHER.)

5. Write out a prayer asking God to help you grow in fellowship with Him in prayer. Ask Him also to teach you how to partner with Him in prayer.

6. Read Psalm 40:5 in your Bible and underline it. In light of this verse, can we ever run out of things to praise God for? _____. Write out a prayer thanking Him that there is no end to His goodness.

7. Read Romans 5:8 in your Bible and underline it. What is the greatest reason why we should express our love to the Lord? _____
   _____.
   Write out a prayer below praising God for the truth expressed in this Scripture.

8. When we don't pray, it implies that we think we can
   _____.

But the truth is we can't _____
_____. We need God for _____.
(See page 45, fourth paragraph, in THE POWER OF
PRAYING TOGETHER.) Write out a prayer telling God all
the ways you need Him.

9. Read Genesis 1:27-28 and Psalm 115:16 in your Bible
   and underline them. According to these verses, God
   has given the responsibility for governing earth's
   affairs to whom? _____. Can we
   do this *without* Him? _____. What did
   He specifically say to do? _____
   _____
   _____. Explain how and why we need to
   partner with God to affect what happens on earth.
   (See page 47, first three paragraphs, in THE POWER OF
   PRAYING TOGETHER.)

10. Read Psalm 145:18-19 in your Bible and underline these verses. Whose prayers will God hear? What will He do when He hears your prayers?

11. Do you ever find it difficult to pray? _____. Explain why or why not. Include any of the reasons people find praying difficult listed in bold on pages 48-51 in THE POWER OF PRAYING TOGETHER, if they reflect your feelings.

12. Read 1 John 3:22 and 5:14-15 in your Bible and underline them. Explain in your own words what these verses speak to you about God hearing and answering your prayers.

13. Read Ephesians 3:20-21 in your Bible and underline these verses. In light of this section of Scripture, how much do you think your prayers can accomplish? Why?

14. Read Luke 11:5-8 in your Bible and underline these verses. What do these verses speak to you about praying to God? What are you supposed to do? What will God do?

15. Read Matthew 7:7-8 and Colossians 4:2 and underline them. In light of these Scriptures, what are you supposed to do with regard to prayer? Write your answer out as a prayer to God, asking Him to help you do these things. (For example, "Lord, show me how to ask of You and trust that when I ask I will receive from You...")

Read Chapter 2(b): "The Power of One"
(pages 54-70) from
THE POWER OF PRAYING TOGETHER

1. Read 2 Corinthians 6:18 in your Bible and underline it. Write out a prayer below telling God what it means to you that He is your heavenly Father. (See page 56, Step 1, in THE POWER OF PRAYING TOGETHER.)

2. Read John 9:31 in your Bible and underline it. What is the reward for someone who worships God and lives His way? _____.
   Write out a prayer of praise to God for who He is and

all He has done for you. List as many things as you can think of to praise Him for specifically in your life. (See page 56, Step 2, in THE POWER OF PRAYING TOGETHER.)

3. Read Psalm 18:1-3 in your Bible and underline these verses. Write out a prayer of praise to God listing all the things you can find in these three verses for which we should praise Him. (See page 58, Step 3, in THE POWER OF PRAYING TOGETHER.)

4. Read Proverbs 3:5-6 in your Bible and underline these verses. Write them out as a prayer surrendering your day to the Lord. (For example, "Lord, I surrender my day to You and commit to trust in You with all my heart..." See page 58, Step 4, in THE POWER OF PRAYING TOGETHER.)

5. Read Romans 12:1 in your Bible and underline it. Write out this verse as a prayer to God presenting your body to Him for His glory. (For example, "Lord, I present my body to you as a living sacrifice..." See page 60, Step 5, in THE POWER OF PRAYING TOGETHER.)

6. Read Psalm 66:18-19, Psalm 51:1-2, and 1 John 1:8-9 in your Bible and underline them. What happens to your prayer life when you have unconfessed sin? _____

_____. What happens when you confess your sins? _____

_____. Write

out a prayer asking God to show you any sin in your life that needs to be confessed. Confess anything He reveals to you so your prayers will not be hindered. (See page 61, Step 6, in The Power of Praying Together.)

7. Read Matthew 12:34-37 and Psalm 51:10 in your Bible and underline them. Write these verses as a prayer asking God to give you a clean heart so that everything coming from your mouth will be a blessing to you and to others. (See page 62, Step 7, in The Power of Praying Together.)

8. Read Matthew 6:31-33 in your Bible and underline these verses. What do they say about praying for what you need? Write out a prayer telling God all of your needs today. (See page 63, Step 8, in The Power of Praying Together.)

9. Read Colossians 1:9-10 in your Bible and underline these verses. Write them out as a prayer asking God to keep you in His will. (For example, "Lord, I pray that You would fill me with the knowledge of Your will in all wisdom..." See page 63, Step 9, in THE POWER OF PRAYING TOGETHER.)

10. The Bible instructs us to "pray for one another" (James 5:16). Write out a prayer for the people who are part of your life. Be specific about their needs. (See page 64, Step 10, in THE POWER OF PRAYING TOGETHER.)

11. In what ways would you like to see your prayer life change? _____

_____

_____. What could you do to establish better prayer habits? _____

_____. What

are two ways to increase the power of your prayers when you pray? Explain and then write out a prayer asking God to help you accomplish those things. (See pages 64-65 in THE POWER OF PRAYING TOGETHER.)

12. Read John 15:7 in your Bible and underline it. What does this verse say to you about receiving answers to your prayers?

13. Read Luke 11:13 and 12:32 in your Bible and underline them. How does God feel about giving to you? How does that make you feel regarding your prayer life?

14. Read 2 Chronicles 16:9 in your Bible and underline it. How do you think the Lord feels about answering your prayers?

15. Read the prayer on pages 67-69 in THE POWER OF PRAYING TOGETHER out loud. Include specifics about your own life. List below the parts of the prayer you most need God to answer.

Read Chapter 3(a): "Finding a Partner"
(pages 71-84) from
THE POWER OF PRAYING TOGETHER

1. Read James 5:16 again in your Bible. What are we sup-
posed to do for one another? _____
_____. Why?
_____.
What kind of prayer does God want? _____
_____.

2. Read James 1:22-25 in your Bible and underline these
verses. Explain in your own words what they say to do.
In light of *this* section of Scripture, what does it mean
we should be doing with regard to James 5:16 above?

3. Read 2 Corinthians 3:18 in your Bible and underline it. Do you think God wants you to grow or stay the way you are? _____

_____.

Write out a prayer below asking God to help you grow into a powerful person of prayer.

4. Read Matthew 18:19 in your Bible and underline it. What is the promise to you in this Scripture? How does it make you feel with regard to praying with another person?

5. On pages 71-79 in THE POWER OF PRAYING TOGETHER, prayer circles are described. Have you ever been in a situation where you were called upon to pray out loud for someone you didn't know? If so, describe that experience. How did you feel about it before, during, and afterward? Was it a positive or negative experience? Explain why. If you have never done anything like that, explain how you think you would feel if you

were called upon to pray out loud for someone you did not know. Do you feel you are prepared or unprepared?

6. Read Isaiah 6:8 in your Bible and underline it. Do you feel you can say these same words to the Lord with regard to praying with and for other people? Can you say, "Here I am, Lord. Send *me* to the prayer closet to pray for them." In other words, if you knew God was looking for someone who would pray for a specific person, would you volunteer to be the one to pray or would you hesitate? _____.
Write out a prayer asking God to help you always be willing to pray for whomever He puts on your heart.

7. Read 1 Timothy 2:1 in your Bible and underline it. Write out a prayer asking God to help you do what this verse says to do. In other words, ask God to help you learn to pray for other people. Tell Him of any way in which you feel reluctant, fearful, or hesitant about doing this.

8. Read 2 Corinthians 1:3-4 in your Bible and underline these verses. What does God do for us? _____
_____
_____.

What are we to do then? _____
_____
_____.

Pastor Jack said to "come _____ of people, don't come ____ them. Be _____ and not _____. The word for 'comfort' in Greek is *paraklesis,* which means to _____ _____ because _____ _____." (See page 82, first paragraph, in THE POWER OF PRAYING TOGETHER.) In light of 2 Corinthians 1:3-4, and also what Pastor Jack said, describe how we are supposed to pray for others. Write out a prayer asking God to help you pray that way for other people.

9. Read Jeremiah 17:14 and 30:17, Psalm 103:2-3, Isaiah 53:5, and Malachi 4:2 in your Bible and underline them. One of the prayers you will be asked to pray most often for other people will be for healing. Write out a prayer asking God for healing for someone you know who needs it and incorporate these Scriptures into the prayer. (For example, "Lord, I know if You heal someone, they will be healed. Thank You that Your Word says You will restore health to us and...")

10. Read Romans 8:37 in your Bible and underline it. Write out a prayer for someone who is suffering in some way, and thank God for the specific promise included in this verse.

11. Read Romans 4:19-21 in your Bible and underline these verses. What do they say about Abraham's belief in the promises of God? Write out a prayer asking God to give you the same kind of faith Abraham had when you pray.

12. Look up the following Scriptures in your Bible and underline the words that describe what we are to do for one another. Write those words below.

Ezekiel 24:23

Mark 9:50

Romans 12:10

Romans 15:7

1 Corinthians 12:25

Galatians 5:13

Ephesians 4:2

13. Look up the following verses in your Bible and underline the words that tell you what you should do for others. Write what you have underlined as a *prayer* asking God to help you do these things. (For example, under Ephesians 4:32 you might write, "Lord, help me to be kind and tenderhearted toward others...")

Ephesians 4:32

Ephesians 5:21

1 Thessalonians 5:11

Hebrews 10:24

1 Peter 1:22

1 Peter 3:8

1 Peter 4:10

14. Look up the following verses in your Bible and underline the words that describe what we should never do to one another. Write them out below.

Leviticus 19:11

Leviticus 25:14,17

Leviticus 25:46

James 5:9

Matthew 24:10

15. Look up the following verses in your Bible and underline them. Write them out below as a prayer asking God to keep you from ever doing any of these things. (For example, "Lord, help me never to wrong another person"—Acts 7:26.)

Acts 7:26

Romans 1:27

Romans 14:13

Joel 2:8

1 Corinthians 6:7

Week Six

Read Chapter 3(b): "Finding a Partner"
(pages 84-95) from
THE POWER OF PRAYING TOGETHER

1. Read 1 Peter 4:7-9 in your Bible and underline verse 8. Explain how this verse could guide you in praying with a prayer partner.

2. Read Romans 14:13 again in your Bible. Write a prayer below asking God to help you not sit in judgment or be critical of anyone with whom you are praying.

3. Read Colossians 3:14 in your Bible and underline it. What is the greatest thing we can do for another person? _____. Write out a prayer asking God to help you be motivated by love for others in all that you do, especially when you pray.

4. Do you have a prayer partner? _____. Have you ever had a person in your life with whom you can pray on a regular basis? _____. If you said yes to either of these questions, describe your experience. Has it been a positive one? Why or why not? Would you want to have another prayer partner? If you answered no to either of the first two questions above, how do you feel about having a person in your life with whom you can pray regularly? Is that something you want or don't want? Give the reasons for your answer.

5. Read John 14:13-14 in your Bible and underline it. What is the promise to you in this Scripture? _____

_____

_____. Do the words of Jesus in this verse

strengthen your faith? Explain your answer. According to this verse, what do you always need to remember to do when praying with a prayer partner?

6. Read 1 John 1:7 in your Bible and underline it. What is the one thing we need to have in common in order to have fellowship with one another? Why would this be important to remember when choosing a prayer partner?

7. How do you feel about praying out loud in front of and for another person? Do you find it intimidating, easy, frightening, fulfilling? Explain this in a prayer to God and ask Him to help you become a person who prays in power for other people.

8. Read Psalm 138:3 in your Bible and underline it. Write this verse out as a prayer of thanksgiving to God. (For example, "Lord, thank You that when I cry out to You, You will...")

9. Look up Philippians 4:13 in your Bible and underline it. List below any fears you have, or have *had,* about praying out loud in front of someone. Then beside each fear, write the word "but" and then write out this verse.

10. Read Philippians 4:6-7 in your Bible and underline these verses. Write them out as a prayer asking God to help you pray with others. (For example, "Lord, help me to not be anxious about praying with others, but rather...")

11. Is there a time in your life when you remember specifically praying with another person and seeing an answer to prayer or noticing a difference afterward? _____. If you answered yes, describe what happened and how it built your faith. If you answered no, write out a prayer asking God to give you opportunities to pray with others and see life-changing answers to your prayers.

12. Read Matthew 21:22 in your Bible and underline it. Write this verse out as a thankful prayer to God. (For example, "Lord, I thank You that You have said in Your Word that whatever I ask of You in prayer...") Ask God to help you memorize this verse so you can quote it in prayer over others.

13. Have you ever had opportunities to pray with other people that you hesitated to take advantage of? If so, write out a prayer asking God to make you bold enough to take advantage of those kinds of golden opportunities. If you have not seen any possibilities for prayer with another, write out a prayer asking God to bring such opportunities into your life and help you to recognize them.

14. If God can arrange for you to be in a certain place at a certain time in order to pray, why doesn't He just go ahead and arrange for the answer to the prayer without you having to pray at all? (See page 92, top of page, in THE POWER OF PRAYING TOGETHER).

15. Pray the prayer on pages 93-94 in THE POWER OF PRAYING TOGETHER out loud. Include specifics about your own need to have one or more prayer partners. List below the parts of the prayer you most need God to answer.

Read Chapter 4(a): "Join the Group"
(pages 97-111) from
THE POWER OF PRAYING TOGETHER

1. Read Matthew 18:19 again. This time focus on the word "agree." The Greek word for unity is *sumphoneo*, from which we get the word *symphony*. What things do *you* feel must be agreed upon when praying with others so that the group will function in unity and achieve harmony?

2. Read Amos 3:3 in your Bible and underline it. What does this Scripture mean for people who want to pray together as a group? _____
_____. Write out a prayer asking God to bring unity and agreement in prayer whenever you pray with other people.

3. Read Romans 12:16 in your Bible and underline it. Why do you think it is important that the people who are praying together in a group be of the same mind? What other attitude mentioned in this verse is good to have as a member of a prayer group?

4. Read Philippians 2:1-2 in your Bible and underline it. Write this section of Scripture out in your own words. What are these verses saying you should do?

5. Read the following verses in your Bible and underline them if you haven't already. Indicate below each Scripture whether or not you believe this is an important point to agree on when praying with other people. Explain why.

John 14:6

1 John 1:9

1 Corinthians 6:19

2 Timothy 3:16

Hebrews 13:8

6. Read Romans 15:5-6 in your Bible and underline these verses. What is the main reason that we need to be like-minded? _____
_____. Write out these two verses as a prayer that you might pray in a prayer group. (For example, "God of patience and comfort, I ask that You would grant us to be like-minded toward one another...")

7. Are there people in your life who share a major thing in common with you and with whom you could form an affinity prayer group? (For example, people who work at the same place or have the same line of work or who have the same concerns, same situations, same

activities, and so on.) Explain below. Is that something you would enjoy doing? Why or why not? (See pages 109-111 in THE POWER OF PRAYING TOGETHER.)

8. List the advantages of being in an affinity group. (See page 111, first and second paragraphs, in THE POWER OF PRAYING TOGETHER.)

9. What are the challenges of being in an affinity group? (See page 111, third paragraph, in THE POWER OF PRAYING TOGETHER.)

10. Read Philippians 2:3-4 in your Bible and underline these verses. Write them out as a prayer asking God to work their message into your heart and the hearts of

those with whom you pray. (For example, "Lord, whenever I pray with anyone else, let nothing be done through selfish ambition...")

11. Read 1 Samuel 12:23 in your Bible and underline it. In this chapter, Samuel is talking to people who had made wrong choices and sinned against God. He encouraged them to keep following the Lord and do what's right. What does this Scripture say to you about continuing to pray for other people, even when you become frustrated by the way they are living? _____ _____. If you are praying with someone to be set free from some sin or temptation and they keep falling back into it, what are you to do? _____ _____. Are you good at pressing through in prayer for something or someone as long as it takes to see an answer and for God to move in their behalf in some way? _____. Regardless of your answer, write out a prayer asking God to help you persevere in prayer as long as necessary.

12. Read Romans 14:19 in your Bible and underline it. What are we to go after? _____

_____

_____. Why? _____

_____. What happens to people when we build them up? _____

_____. How might someone be built up in a prayer group? How might it bring peace to a prayer group if people can trust that they will be encouraged and edified there, and not criticized, put down, or lectured?

13. Read Colossians 3:15 in your Bible and underline it. Write out a prayer asking for the peace of God to rule your heart in such a powerful way that you bring a spirit of peace to any group of people you are with.

14. Read Colossians 3:12-13 in your Bible and underline these verses. Write them out as a prayer asking God to help you do these things for others. (For example, "Lord, because I am one of Your elect, because I am holy and loved by You, I ask that You would help me to be tender and merciful, filled with kindness...")

15. Read Galatians 6:2 in your Bible and underline it. Explain how this verse might be fulfilled in a prayer group. Write out a prayer asking God to help you do that as you pray for others.

Read Chapter 4(b): "Join the Group"
(pages 111-120) from
THE POWER OF PRAYING TOGETHER

1. Have you been part of a prayer group before? _____.
   If you have, was the experience a positive or a negative
   one? Explain. If you have never been part of a prayer
   group before, explain why.

2. Are you part of a prayer group now, or would you like to be part of a prayer group? _____. Explain your answer and give reasons as to why or why not.

3. Describe the kind of prayer group you would like to be involved in. Or, if you already are involved in one, describe it.

Where do you meet?

How many people are in it?

How often do you meet?

How long are the meetings?

Who is in the group?

4. Read Ephesians 4:25 in your Bible and underline it. Why is it important to be honest with others when we give our requests? _____ _____. While we don't have to tell others *everything* about our personal lives or more than they need to know, why is it important to not pretend something is great in our lives when it really is not?

5. Read Romans 12:10-13 in your Bible. Having already underlined verse 10, now underline verses 11-13. Write all of these verses out in your own words describing what it should be like among the members

of a prayer group or home group. (For example, "As members of a prayer group, we should be kind and affectionate to one another...")

6. List seven guidelines that will help you maintain a successful prayer group. (See pages 114-117 in THE POWER OF PRAYING TOGETHER.) Under each one explain why this is an important thing to do in a prayer group.

1. Have _____.

2. Choose _____.

3. Encourage _____.

4. Don't _____.

5. Stress _____.

6. Don't _____.

7. Do not _____.

7. Which of the above guidelines do you think might be the most difficult for you, from either the perspective of a group leader or as a member of a group? Explain the reasons for your answer. Write out a prayer asking God to help you with that particular aspect when you are involved in group prayer.

8. Write out a list of 10 to 12 people you would like to be in a prayer group with. Write a prayer lifting up these people to the Lord and asking Him to show you if you should initiate a time of prayer with any of them. Ask Him to reveal anyone else you may have not thought about as a potential prayer group member.

9. What are some of the benefits for anyone who is in a prayer group? (See page 117, last paragraph, in THE POWER OF PRAYING TOGETHER.)

10. What are some of the specific reasons that you believe being in a prayer group could be beneficial for *you* personally? What do you need to receive from it? What do you want to give?

11. Read Galatians 6:8-10 in your Bible and underline these verses. How could praying in a group be considered sowing? _____

_____. What kind of sowing would it be? _____

_____. What would you reap? _____

_____. What does verse 9 encourage you to do with regard to pressing through in prayer?

_____

_____.

How does verse 10 support the importance of praying with and for others?

12. Read Acts 2:46 in your Bible and underline it. What did the people in the first church do?

13. Read Acts 1:9-14 in your Bible and underline verse 14. What did Mary, the mother of Jesus, and His brothers and disciples do as a group after He was taken up into heaven? _____

_____

_____ (verse 14). What do you think they might have been praying about? _____

_____.

How could this set a precedent as the first prayer group?

14. Read 1 Corinthians 13:13 in your Bible and underline it. What is the most important thing to remember when being a part of a prayer group or home group?
_____.

   Write out a prayer asking God to help you show love to others at all times, especially when you are in a group situation.

15. Pray the prayer on pages 118-119 in THE POWER OF PRAYING TOGETHER out loud. Include your specific needs with regard to praying in a small group setting. List below the parts of the prayer you most need God to answer.

Week Nine

Read Chapter 5(a): "The Power of a Praying
Church" (Pages 121-137) from
THE POWER OF PRAYING TOGETHER

1. Read Acts 2:41-42 in your Bible and underline verse 42.
   What were the main activities of the first recorded
   Christian church?

2. Read Acts 4:29-31 in your Bible and underline verse 31.
   Describe in your own words what happened in the
   early church as told in these verses. What did they pray
   for? What happened after they prayed?

3. The power of the church is still _____. And we, the _____ _____ _____, can also be shaken by the _____ _____ of _____. We can see things_____ _____ in the world around us if we are _____ to _____ as fervently and as _____ as the early church did, mirroring also their _____ and _____. (See page 125, first paragraph, in THE POWER OF PRAYING TOGETHER.)

4. Are you a member of a church family, one of God's households? _____. If you answered yes, describe where you attend church and how you feel in relation to the other members. Do you feel connected or disconnected? Why? If you answered no, explain why you are not a member of any church family at this time. Have you not found one where you feel at home or welcome? Did you have a negative experience with a church in the past? Explain. Write out a prayer asking God to lead you to the church family He has for you where you can grow and become whole.

5. Read Romans 12:4-5 in your Bible and underline these verses. Do you see the members of your church as your spiritual family? _____. If you answered yes, describe how you feel about them and why you feel connected. If you answered no, write out a prayer asking God to help you feel connected to the spiritual family where you are, or place you in a church body that will be a spiritual family to you.

6. Read the following Scriptures in your Bible and underline the words that describe how we, the body of Christ, are to be. Write those words below.

1 Corinthians 12:12

Ephesians 4:14-16

Colossians 2:18-19

1 Corinthians 1:10

What is the common thread among all of the above verses?

7. Explain the difference between the *omnipresence*, the *promise presence*, and the *manifest presence* of God. (See page 126, first and second paragraphs, in THE POWER OF PRAYING TOGETHER.)

Omnipresence of God

Promise Presence of God

Manifest Presence of God

8. How does a church build a house for God's manifest presence? _____
_____. What happens when the church welcomes God's presence in praise and worship? _____
_____. What happens when we *don't* welcome God's presence in worship? _____
_____.

How does a congregation make a choice as to what degree they want the presence of God in their midst?

_____

_____. (See page 126, third and fourth paragraphs, in THE POWER OF PRAYING TOGETHER.)

9. Read 1 Peter 2:4-5 in your Bible and underline these verses. As we come to the Lord, what are we to become and what are we to do?

10. The church is not just a building, the church is the _____. People who believe in Jesus make up the _____. The church _____ is a place where believers can _____ to be _____ _____, _____, and prepared to go out and do _____ _____. (See page 128, third paragraph, in THE POWER OF PRAYING TOGETHER.) Do you feel you are being nurtured and prepared to go out and do God's work? Why or why not?

11. Everyone in the church—the body of _____,
    the _____ has a _____ for
    their _____. And God has placed _____,
    _____ and _____ in
    each one of us in order to _____
    that _____. Belonging to a _____—
    a local _____ of _____ a
    _____—led by godly _____
    who will help you _____, is the most effective
    way to _____ and _____ those gifts
    and become an _____ _____ _____
    for God's _____. Through this _____
    _____, God will teach you about _____
    and His _____ for your _____. (See page
    128, last paragraph, in THE POWER OF PRAYING
    TOGETHER.)

12. Do you feel that when you go to church, something
    discernible is happening in you and you are growing?
    _____. Do you feel refreshed, renewed, encour-
    aged, and edified? _____. If you answered yes to
    these questions, write out a prayer of thanksgiving to
    God for that and ask Him to continue to bless your
    congregation and your pastor and leaders. If you said
    no to either of these questions, write out a prayer
    asking God to pour out His Spirit on your church so
    that it will become a life-giving, dynamic, edifying
    spiritual family. Ask Him to enable you to receive all
    He has for you there.

13. It is impossible to _____ and _____
    to your fullest _____ independently
    of _____ _____. (See page 130,
    third paragraph, in THE POWER OF PRAYING TOGETHER.)
    Building a people to do _____ _____
    happens in the local _____ when we are
    _____ to and _____ with the
    rest of the _____. It is within
    that context that we find ____ we are_____ to
    be and what we are _____ to _____.
    One of the most important things about being in a
    spiritual _____ is finding _____ in
    _____ through _____. When the *leaders*
    are in _____, and the _____
    are in _____ with them and with _____
    _____, there is a dynamic that
    adds _____ to their _____ and the
    _____ that God will _____
    in _____. (See page 131, first and second para-
    graphs.)

14. Have you ever prayed for something as part of a con-
    gregation in corporate prayer that was answered pow-
    erfully by the Lord? _____. If you answered yes,
    describe one such situation and write out a prayer
    asking God to enable the congregation you are in to
    pray in greater power than ever before. If you

answered no, write out a prayer asking God to make your church into a powerful praying church that becomes an irresistible force when it prays.

15. Read Hebrews 10:24-25 in your Bible and underline these verses. Write them out as a prayer to God for yourself and the church family you belong to now, or will belong to in the future. (For example, "Lord, I pray that I and the members of my church and spiritual family will be considerate of one another so that we can...")

Read Chapter 5(b): "The Power of a Praying
Church" (pages 137-153) from
THE POWER OF PRAYING TOGETHER

1. Read John 13:34-35 in your Bible and underline these
   verses. How are we supposed to act toward one
   another? _____
   _____. What should be our
   attitude? _____
   _____. Do you believe these
   verses are talking only about how you relate to people
   in your own church? How should we act toward the
   members of other churches and Christian denominations?

2. Read Ephesians 2:14 in your Bible and underline it. The
   New King James Version says that Jesus, who is our
   peace, "has broken down the middle wall of separation."

If these words imply unity and a ceasing of hostility, how should we relate to people from other churches and denominations? Why?

3. Read Matthew 5:9 in your Bible and underline it. Are you aware of any serious divisions within a church or between different denominations? _____. Are you aware of any critical attitudes among some people toward members of other churches or denominations? _____. If you answered yes to either question, write out a prayer explaining the problem before God and asking Him to bring peace, healing, and understanding to the situation. If you answered no to both questions, write out a prayer asking God to bring peace wherever there are critical divisions among believers in churches or denominations. Ask Him to make you a peacemaker whenever and wherever possible. (Peacemakers can accomplish much good through prayer.)

4. Read Hebrews 12:14-15 in your Bible and underline these verses. In light of this section of Scripture, what should be our attitude toward people of other races and cultures? Why? What will happen if we don't pursue peace with people who are of a different race or culture than we are?

5. Read 1 Peter 3:8-12 in your Bible and underline these verses. What are we supposed to do for others? What could be the consequences for us if we do not treat people of other cultures and races with love and respect?

6. Read Matthew 5:23-24 in your Bible and underline these verses. What could hinder the power of our prayers?

7. Write out a prayer asking God to reveal to you if there is anything of prejudice in you regarding any race or culture for any reason. If He shows you something, confess it and ask Him to set you completely free of it.

8. Write out a prayer asking God to use you to help break down attitudes of hatred, animosity, separation,

or disrespect toward other races or cultures in your neighborhood, workplace, community, city, state, or places where you go. Write down anything He shows you to do.

9. In order for there to come reconciliation, there must first come intercession. Write out a prayer asking God to break down any walls of separation within your church and within the churches of your city. Ask Him to make every one of them praying churches and His instruments of reconciliation and healing for people of other races and cultures.

10. Does your church or any church in your area have meetings to pray for your city? _____. If you answered yes, write out a prayer asking God to bless those prayer times and increase the attendance at those meetings. If you answered no, write out a prayer asking God to put on the hearts of pastors and leaders to organize times to pray for your city. Ask Him to use you as an instrument to in some way help make that happen, whether as an intercessor or in some other practical way.

11. Read Leviticus 26:8 in your Bible and underline it. In light of this Scripture, why do you think it's important for individual churches to organize times for their congregation to gather to pray? Why would it be important for churches to join together in city-wide prayer meetings? What could happen if they did?

12. Read Jeremiah 29:7 in your Bible and underline it. In light of this Scripture, what should we be doing?

_____

_____

_____. Write out five ways you and others could pray in order to see greater peace come to your city.

1.

2.

3.

4.

5.

13. Look up the following verses and write below what the people of this early Christian church did together.

    Acts 2:1

    Acts 4:24

    Acts 5:12

    What is the common thread in these three verses?

14. What are two things we need to do in order to be of "one accord" as a praying church or a praying group of believers? (See page 149, first paragraph, in THE POWER OF PRAYING TOGETHER.)

    1.

    2.

15. Pray the prayer on pages 150-152 in THE POWER OF PRAYING TOGETHER. Include specifics about your own church, community, and city. List below the parts of the prayer you most desire God to answer.

Read Chapter 6(a): "Uniting in Prayer to
Move a Nation" (pages 155-165) from
THE POWER OF PRAYING TOGETHER

1. Read 2 Chronicles 7:14 in your Bible and underline it.
   What are four things God asks us, His children, to do?

   1.

   2.

   3.

   4.

If we will do those things, what are the three things God promises to do?

1.

2.

3.

2. Read 1 Timothy 2:1-4 in your Bible and underline the verses not yet underlined. What are we supposed to be doing with regard to our president and our leaders? Why?

3. Based on 1 Timothy 2:1-4, what are three important things we should remember? (See page 157, first paragraph, in THE POWER OF PRAYING TOGETHER.)

   1. (verse 1)

   2. (verse 2)

   3. (verses 3 and 4)

4. Read Proverbs 29:2 in your Bible and underline it. In light of this Scripture, why should we pray about our leaders? What could happen if we don't?

5. An intercessor is someone who _____ into the
   _____ between God's _____
   and man's _____, and through
   _____, brings the merits of the
   _____ to bear upon _____ and
   _____. (See page 159,
   last paragraph, in THE POWER OF PRAYING TOGETHER.)
   Intercessors are needed because the world is filled
   with _____ and _____ who don't
   understand the _____ of their own
   _____. Or they don't _____
   _____ everything God can ____ ____
   _____, and so they don't know to _____
   for _____. They
   don't realize the _____ of _____ _____
   for them, so they need someone who will _____
   into their _____ in
   _____. (See page 160, first paragraph.)

6. Read Ezekiel 22:30-31 in your Bible and underline
   these verses. Why are they two of the saddest verses
   in the Bible? (See page 160, second, third, and fourth
   paragraphs.)

7. Read Jeremiah 18:7-10 in your Bible and underline
   verses 8 and 10. What happens when a nation stops
   doing evil things? _____
   _____.

What happens when a nation does evil and does not obey God's laws? _____

_____

_____.

8. In light of Jeremiah 18:7-10, how should we be praying for our nation? _____

_____

_____.

Write out a prayer below confessing the sins of our nation and asking God to help us become a people who live His way.

9. What are the specific sins of your nation that you would most like to see stopped? Write out a prayer below asking God to put an end to this kind of sin and disobedience in your land.

10. Read Isaiah 59:1-2 in your Bible and underline these verses. What happens as the result of sin?

11. Read James 4:2 in your Bible and underline it. Can you think of anything in your nation that you have complained about or thought critically about, yet have not prayed about? _____. (Don't feel bad if you have, because we have all done that at one time or another.) If you answered yes, write out a prayer about that particular thing. If you answered no, write out a prayer asking God to reveal to you anything you need to be praying about regarding your nation.

12. Read 2 Kings 6:14-17 in your Bible and underline verse 16. Describe what happened in these verses. Write out a prayer asking God to open the eyes of your understanding to see how He protects you and the people you pray about, and also your nation when people intercede for it.

13. Read Luke 19:13 in your Bible and underline it. If God wants us to do business until He comes and the business of the church is prayer, what should we be doing daily? _____. Write out a prayer asking God to open your eyes to different ways to pray for your nation. Write down anything He reveals to you.

14. We are supposed to ask _____ for things that we
    see need to _____, not because *He* _____
    _____ _____, but because He has
    _____ us as
    _____—people who _____
    _____ _____ on behalf of _____
    _____ to invoke _____ _____
    and grace. And that is never more clear than in
    _____ to our _____. (See page
    164, last paragraph, in THE POWER OF PRAYING
    TOGETHER.)

15. Write out a prayer asking God to make you into an
    intercessor for our nation. Ask Him to show you how
    you can join with *others* to pray for the nation as well.
    Write down anything He shows you.

Read Chapter 6(b): "Uniting in Prayer to
Move a Nation" (pages 165-180) from
THE POWER OF PRAYING TOGETHER

1. Read Nehemiah 1:3-4 in your Bible and underline these
   verses. How did Nehemiah react when he saw that the
   wall around his city was broken down and its gates
   destroyed? _____
   _____
   _____. What could we do to see the wall
   of God's protection around our nation built up?

2. Nehemiah's concern for the _____ of the
   _____ motivated him to _____.
   Our_____ for the _____ in our
   nation should _____ us to
   _____ too. We need to be so _____
   _____ over the _____
   _____ of _____ that we

99

think _____ about their _____
than we do about____ _____.
(See page 166, first paragraph, in THE POWER OF
PRAYING TOGETHER.)

3. Read Psalm 127:1 in your Bible and underline it. In
   light of this verse, how can you pray about our nation?

4. Do you have a sense that God is calling people across
   the land to pray for the nation? _____. If you
   answered yes, write out a prayer telling God you
   sense in His Word and in your spirit that He is calling
   you to pray along with many others for your nation.
   Ask Him to show you *how* to pray. Ask Him to lead
   many others to hear that call too. If you answered no,
   write out a prayer asking God to help you hear His
   call to pray and to teach you how to move into intercessory prayer for your nation.

5. Read Nehemiah 1:5-10 in your Bible and underline verses 6 and 9. What did Nehemiah do on behalf of the people of Israel? _____

_____

_____

(verse 6). What did he say the people of Israel had done? _____

_____

_____ (verse 7).
What did God promise to do if the people returned to Him and kept His commandments? _____

_____

_____

(verse 9).

6. In light of Nehemiah 1:5-10, how should you pray for your nation? Write that out as a prayer to God below.

7. One of the most important things Nehemiah did as he _____ the _____ of the _____ and the _____ was to _____ the _____ of the _____. God is asking _____ to do the _____. God wants our _____ to _____ for the _____ of our _____ too. He

wants us to _____ _____
before _____ and _____ the _____
of our _____ so He can _____ the
_____ in the _____ of our
_____. (See page 170, second paragraph, in
THE POWER OF PRAYING TOGETHER.)

8. Instead of letting the moral decay in our country get
   us down, Pastor Jack advises us to "focus on the
   promises of God, and not on the _____;
   focus on the Savior's _____, and not on the
   _____ _____; focus on our
   privilege in _____, and not on our
   _____; focus on _____
   in _____, and not on anger over
   surrounding _____; and focus on identifying
   with the _____, and not on their _____
   or _____." (See page 171, first paragraph,
   in THE POWER OF PRAYING TOGETHER.)

9. While we need to _____ the sin, we don't
   need to _____ on the sin. We should instead
   focus on the _____, who needs to be _____
   of his _____ by coming to the _____, and
   we should do so without condescension or _____
   _____ of attitude, but with _____
   _____ and _____.
   (See page 171, first paragraph, in THE POWER OF
   PRAYING TOGETHER.)

10. Read James 5:19-20 in your Bible and underline these verses. Keeping in mind that we are a sinful and rebellious people who don't want to acknowledge God or live His way, write out a prayer confessing those particular sins of our nation, seeking God's forgiveness for them, and asking Him to turn the hearts of the people in this nation away from sin.

11. Read Ephesians 6:12 in your Bible and underline it. In light of this Scripture, who is our real enemy?

12. Read 2 Corinthians 10:3-4 and Ephesians 6:17-18 in your Bible and underline them. In light of these verses, how are we supposed to wage war? _____

_____

_____

_____.

What are our greatest spiritual weapons? _____
_____
_____
_____.

How are we to do warfare on behalf of other believers? _____
_____
_____.

13. Read Deuteronomy 20:3-4 in your Bible and underline these verses. How are we supposed to feel with regard to our enemies who wage war against us?
_____
_____.

Why are we not to be afraid of our enemies? _____
_____
_____.

Who or what do you feel is the greatest threat to our nation? _____
_____
_____.

Write out a prayer below asking God to be with our nation in the fight against the enemy.

14. Read 1 Thessalonians 5:16-18 in your Bible and underline these verses. Write them out as a prayer to God asking Him to help you do what they say to do, especially with regard to your country. (For example, "Lord, I pray that You would help me to continually rejoice over the wonderful things about my country and the great things You have done and are doing in it...")

15. Pray the prayer on pages 176-179 in THE POWER OF PRAYING TOGETHER out loud. Include specifics about your own nation. List below the parts of the prayer you most need God to answer.

Read Chapter 7(a): "What in the World Can
I Do?" (pages 181-195) from
THE POWER OF PRAYING TOGETHER

1. How do you feel about praying for people and situations in other parts of the world? Does it seem monumental, intimidating, or overwhelming to you? Do you believe your prayers have power when you pray for people in remote parts of the world? Why? Explain your answers.

2. Do you make it a regular practice to pray about situations and people around the world? _____. If you answered yes, what things do you usually pray about? How would you like to grow as an intercessor for the world? Write out your answer as a prayer to God. If you

answered no, write out a prayer asking God to give you the heart and knowledge you need to pray for the world.

3. Read Romans 8:26 in your Bible and underline it. How does this verse make you feel with regard to praying for big issues in the world? Does it take the pressure off? In what way? Explain.

4. Write out a prayer asking God to speak to you with regard to how *He* wants you to specifically pray for the world. Ask Him to make you sensitive to the leading and enablement of the Holy Spirit as you pray.

5. Read Luke 17:5-6 in your Bible and underline these verses. What did the disciples ask Jesus to do for them? _____ _____. In your own words, what did Jesus say to them about faith? _____ _____ _____ _____.

Write out a prayer asking God for the same thing the disciples asked Jesus for.

6. Read Jeremiah 1:10 in your Bible and underline it. In light of this Scripture, what do you think is God's attitude with regard to us praying for other nations of the world? What can we accomplish?

7. Read Psalm 2:8 in your Bible and underline it. What does God ask us to do? _____

_____

_____

_____.

In light of this verse, what could happen if you were to adopt a particular nation in prayer and regularly pray for God to pour out His Spirit on the people in that nation so that they would turn to the Lord?

8. God wants to pour out _____ _____ on all _____ so they can be brought to a _____ of _____. He promises to give us the _____ we ask for—even people groups who seem to be _____ _____ to reach with the _____ about _____. God has not forsaken the _____ of the earth. We have forsaken our _____ to _____. But as we _____ to what the Lord is _____ us to _____ about, no matter how big or impossible it may seem, there is no _____ to what _____ will _____. (See page 193, second paragraph, in THE POWER OF PRAYING TOGETHER.)

9. What nation has God put specifically on your heart to pray for? _____.
   What in particular in that nation do you feel especially led to pray about? If you don't have a nation in mind, write out a prayer asking God to bring to your mind and heart a nation to pray for on a consistent basis.

10. Tell in your own words how intercessory prayer can be compared to a football game. (See page 192, first and second paragraphs, in THE POWER OF PRAYING TOGETHER.)

11. Can you think of a situation in the world that needs to be intercepted in prayer and turned around and headed another way? Explain.

12. In light of your answer above, how could you seize that particular situation in prayer? Write out your answer as a prayer below.

13. Read James 5:16 in your Bible again. The last part of this verse describes *how* you are supposed to pray for people, situations, and conditions in the world and what happens when you do. Write out a fervent prayer below about the issue in the world that you feel most passionate about. Pray this prayer often during the next month.

14. What is one of the meanings of the word "intercede"?

_____

_____. (See page 193, last paragraph, in THE POWER OF PRAYING TOGETHER.) Have you ever had something happen *to* you or *around* you and you sensed it was not just by accident that you were there? Did you feel you were called to intercede in the situation? _____. If you answered yes, explain what happened and how you reacted to it. If you answered no, write out a prayer asking God to show you whenever you are in certain situations at strategic times as His intercessor.

15. Can you think of a situation right now that you have knowledge of, are touched by, or are in the midst of, where God may possibly have you there for the purpose of interceding about this matter? _____.
If you answered yes, write out a prayer of intercession regarding that situation. If you answered no, write out a prayer asking God to reveal to you anyone or anything He specifically wants you to pray about right now. Ask Him to raise up other intercessors besides you to pray about it as well.

Week Fourteen

Read Chapter 7(b): "What in the World Can
I Do?" (pages 195-204) from
THE POWER OF PRAYING TOGETHER

1. Read 2 Samuel 22:7-8 in your Bible and underline these
   verses. How do you think the prayers of God's people
   could possibly affect the world? Do you think they
   could shake things up a bit?

2. Read Mark 11:17 in your Bible and underline it. What
   does Jesus say God's house should be called? _____
   _____.
   What is one of the main duties of believers in the
   church?

3. Read Matthew 28:19 in your Bible and underline it. What is the last commandment Jesus gave His disciples and us? _____

_____

_____. How can we help see that accomplished through prayer? In what ways can we pray?

4. Read Psalm 67:1-4 in your Bible and underline these verses. Write out a prayer for the nations of the world inspired by this psalm.

5. Can you think of a situation in the world that you would like to be a part of seeing changed through intercessory prayer? Describe that situation in a prayer to God asking Him to intervene. Ask Him to raise up other intercessors like yourself with a heart to pray for this too.

6. Are you a member of any kind of group who prays for global concerns? _____. If you answered yes, describe that group and what you pray for. If you answered no, write out a prayer asking God to bring such a group into your life.

7. Read Luke 18:27 in your Bible and underline it. Do you feel you can pray beyond yourself and see God answer your prayer? What situation in the world do you especially need to be able to pray beyond your ability and knowledge now? Explain.

8. Read Mark 11:22-24 in your Bible and underline these verses. What does this section of Scripture speak to you with regard to praying for situations around the world? _____

_____
_____. Using the principles in these verses, choose a major world concern that is on your heart and address it in prayer the way Jesus teaches us to do.

9. Read James 1:6-7 in your Bible and underline these verses. How are we supposed to ask for things from God? _____

_____. What happens when we have doubt? _____

_____
_____. Which way do you pray? _____

_____. Write out a prayer asking God to help you have the faith to believe for the answers every time you pray.

10. Read Romans 4:19-21 in your Bible and underline these verses. How did Abraham react to promises from God? How are *you* supposed to react to God's promises?

11. Read John 4:35-36 in your Bible and underline these verses. What does Jesus want us to see? _____ _____. How can you help with the harvest of souls by praying? ___ _____ _____.

    What would be the result of praying for people to receive the Lord? _____ _____ _____.

12. Read Matthew 9:36-38 in your Bible and underline these verses. Why was Jesus moved with compassion for the people? _____

_____. What did Jesus tell us to pray for? _____

_____.Why did He say that? _____

_____. How should our heart be when praying for the lost?

13. Read Revelation 5:9 in your Bible and underline it. Whom did Jesus want to redeem when He died on the cross? _____

_____. In light of this Scripture, do we need to pray for people all over the world to be saved? _____. Write out a prayer asking God to redeem the souls of a particular people group whom you know to be unsaved.

14. Read Psalm 46:10 and 47:8 in your Bible and underline these verses. In light of these Scriptures, what is true about God in the nations of the earth? _____

_____

_____

_____. Write out a prayer asking that God be lifted up and exalted among all the nations of the earth.

15. Pray the prayer on pages 201-203 in THE POWER OF PRAYING TOGETHER out loud. Include specifics about your own situation with regard to praying for the world. List below the parts of the prayer that you most desire God to answer.

Answers to Prayer

What answers to prayer have you seen since you started praying with and for other people? What prayers have you seen answered for yourself in your daily devotional prayer time? Record them here. It's important to acknowledge what God has done and praise Him for it.

_____

_____

_____

_____

_____

_____

_____

_____

_____

_____

_____

_____

_____

_____

Answers to Prayer

Answers to Prayer

Answers to Prayer

_____

_____

_____

_____

_____

_____

_____

_____

_____

_____

_____

_____

_____

_____

_____

_____

_____

_____

_____

Answers to Prayer

_____

_____

_____

_____

_____

_____

_____

_____

_____

_____

_____

_____

_____

_____

_____

_____

_____

_____

_____

Answers to Prayer

_____

_____

_____

_____

_____

_____

_____

_____

_____

_____

_____

_____

_____

_____

_____

_____

_____

_____

_____

Answers to Prayer

Answers to Prayer

Other Books by
Stormie Omartian

The Power of a Praying® Husband
Also: Prayer and Study Guide ~ Audiobook ~ Prayer Pak

The Power of a Praying® Nation

The Power of a Praying® Parent
Also: Prayer and Study Guide ~ Audiobook ~ Prayer Cards ~
Prayer Journal

The Power of a Praying® Wife
Also: Prayer and Study Guide ~ Audiobook ~ Prayer Cards ~
Prayer Journal

The Power of a Praying® Woman
Also: Prayer and Study Guide ~ Audiobook ~ Prayer Cards ~
Prayer Journal

The Power of Praying® Together
Also: Prayer and Study Guide ~ Audiobook ~ Prayer Cards ~
Prayer Journal

The Power of Christmas Prayer™

Stormie

Just Enough Light for the Step I'm On
Also: Devotional Prayer Journey ~ Prayer Cards